POEMS OF AN OLD SOLDIER

POEMS OF AN OLD SOLDIER

Bill Jackman

Jackman Publications

First edition published by Jackman Publications

A catalogue record of this book is
available from the British Library.

First edition 2012

ISBN: 978-0-9569098-8-6

Printed and bound in Great Britain by
Lightning Source UK Ltd,
Chapter House, Pitfield, Kiln Farm,
Milton Keynes MK11 3LW

Contents

Foreword

These poems are written
to amuse the public in general,
and in many cases do not conform
to any particular rhythm, rhyme, metre,
pentameter or other poetic jargon.
My apology to the real poets.
Nevertheless, enjoy.

Help for Heroes

The proceeds of this book will
be donated to Help for Heroes

Dedication

I would like to dedicate this book to
Phillip John and Shelagh Marie Jackman

Bill Jackman
Weston-super-Mare
March 2012

1   Royal Wootton Bassett

Dressed in black, she stands alone with her memories, barely conscious of the hundreds of other mourners surrounding her. In her hand she holds a solitary rose.

She is straining hard to retain the salty tears of love and grief that flow unchecked down powdered cheeks. A twelve-month bride and mother to be, what future for her and their child now she is without the man. she loved so very much.

Crowds of men, women and children stand reverently, most of them weeping, some sobbing loudly as the motorcade draws near. This act of grief has no rehearsal, no written invite to attend but she knew she had to come today.

Grown men stand with tear-filled eyes, and salute the flag-covered contents of black stately vehicles as they slowly and reverently pass them by. The flags are lowered in reverence.

As the car bearing her husbands body draws opposite her, she steps forward and kisses her rose before throwing it like a dart onto the centre of the roof where dozens of other flowers were accumulating from unknown well wishers.

It was at that moment she knew she was not alone. These hundreds of people who have come here today are all strangers. It is her husband who is the fallen hero today. It's pouring with rain, so what? These nameless friends and supporters know and understand her grief.

She whispers goodbye. The flags of the Royal British Legion, and from her husband's regiment are now raised, having saluted a lost comrade in arms. It's all over. The sun has come out. People around her are starting to smile and chatter again. Life has stared again.

The crowds are dispersing. She senses a great weight has been lifted from her shoulders. Strangers console her, she is amongst friends. She knows she must be brave for she is not alone any more. She smiles at a friendly, understanding face.

This brave little town of Wootton Bassett, a neighbour to Swindon Town, has lowered its flag for the last time Four years of standing with heads bowed have come to an end. Only the venue of grief has moved on.

When will it end? There is no shortage of replacements .Young men and women know there is a job to be done and dying in its fulfilment is a risk they are prepared to take.

May God find you all a place in heaven if that is your desire.

And you, Wootton Bassett, be content for being the host by being blessed by the Queen with the new name of

Royal Wootton Basset

2   A Tribute to Air Ambulance

Aren't we lucky that there are those who are
Willing to give up their time
To fly a helicopter to inaccessible places
To try and save lives.
Without this service we would be lost,
They carry it out regardless of cost.
At any time night or day
 Conditions permitting they will be on their way

It would have to be bad for them not to fly
To get where you are they certainly try.
No government grants or lottery funds
Are given to help with their task
A small donations from everyone is all they really ask
It costs a lot to fly a chopper,
It has to be maintained as well.
It could be you who they come to next
So buy this book of poems and help the funds swell

3   A Word from Weston Hospice Care

As I lie on my back on my bed in my room
My thoughts once again turn to my family
I shed no tears for the condition I am in
I know it's terminal and there is nothing I can do

But my thoughts go out to my children
Their children and grandchildren too
It's Christmas in two weeks' time
I do hope I last till then, that's all I pray.

It's wonderful the care we receive here
This Hospice was founded in October 89
All colours and religions, rich and poor come here
For relief from pain and enjoying the friendship

The attention given by voluntary dedicated skilled staff
Means that most of us go home cured of cancer
No thanks to Government handouts. All our
Financial help is by voluntary contributions

From all the patients and staff at
Weston-super-Mare Hospice Care
We thank you

4   Two Thousand and Twelve

Christmas is over, the cards must come down
Many have succeeded in their sorrows to drown
Tree decorations are put away until next year
The cost of Christmas more expensive I fear
A new year has started. Good luck to you all
We're going to need it if the euro should fall
Tighten your belts 'cos there's worse to come
Hope Dad keeps his job; and of course Mum
Taxes and strikes are sure to sure to arrive
Let's jolly well hope we can continue to survive
We've come through worse and can do it again
Resist the Credit Crunch, save for when it rains
Next Christmas will soon be here, be sure of that
Let's hope that by then there is no increase in VAT
So despite the gloomy forecast and the Ozone fear
We wish you a Happy and Prosperous New Year

5   Minky

There was a whale named Minky
Who had a great big tail
He liked to splash it in the sea
Though never in a gale

One day he banged it on the rocks
The pain it made him cry
So he went to see his doctor
Who only lived close by

The doctor was a walrus
A jolly gent called Bill
He said that he could help him
And put him on the pill

He had a lovely secretary
Whose name she said was Jade
He asked her to go swimming
She was a qualified mermaid.

They swam across the ocean
Splashing wherever they went
They started up in Bristol
And finished up in Kent

Minky fell in love with Jade
Whose middle name was Midler
Nine months passed then one day
She gave birth to a tiddler

6   Man of the Day

My pal and I had no money,
And the circus was coming to town.
Emptying our pockets we hadn't enough;
We knew we would need half a crown (13p)
So we went and offered our services
To help put up the big top tent
The money I thought we'd get for that
Would buy the tickets and help with Mum's rent

'Keep back,' the man said. 'You are too small.'
He wouldn't let us help out
So me and my mate thought we'd look around
And see what animals were about
We came round this corner, and saw a man
Let a lion out of its cage
We hid, and saw a lion jump out
It seemed confused and in a rage

'What shall we do?' my pal said,
He had gone all sweaty and grey
I said 'You go and get the boss
And I'll keep the lion at bay.'
He didn't need to be asked twice
He went off like a rocket
I was left with the lion
And a ball of string in my pocket

The poor lion didn't know what to do
He let out a mighty roar then he
Turned and jumped back in his cage
And lay on the sawdust floor.
My pal came back with the boss man
Who was very pleased indeed.
He said I was a very brave boy
And could have all the tickets I need

My mum she wouldn't believe me
When I told her what I had done
She took what I said with a pinch of salt
As I was always telling her one
The next day she had to apologise
When she saw what the papers had to say
It said we were both very brave boys
I was the man of the day

7   The Bristol Charger

Monstrous black and invested with the power of the gods
Breathing and hissing softly as he rests. His massive wheels
Of steel are ready to repeat once more that day the long train journey
Back to London where his driver and fireman's homes are located
Replenished with water his tanks now full as is the fender, full of
Chunky black diamonds of coal. A feeling of warmth satisfaction
Overcomes him as his boiler fire is stoked up ready for
The return journey, as if to show his gratitude he lets off a little steam
Just as if he was communicating with his crew that he was rested
And eager to start the journey all over again. They are a team

Extra coaches have been added on. He could pull thirty coaches of
Passengers to their far off destinations and return
It was London rush hour crowds were boarding.
His skin is like a shiny suit of armour. His eight foot long pistons strapped
To either positioned on either side of his body look like
Gleaming lances, over which is his name plate proudly stands
Each letter cut from brass. Large enough so no one will be in
Any doubt he is the famous Bristol Charger.

Time has come to make a move, he's rested and replenished
Now he's ready for departure, all aboard as doors clunk shut
People waving shouting laughing, some weeping as
The whistle is blown. With what appears to be little effort
The Bristol Charger slides smoothly from its darkened
Place of rest into the daylight and the receding sunlight
Clackity clackity clack is heard by everyone as he crosses
The points,effortlesly dragging his tail of carriages behind him

Stations flash by, names hard to read, light grey smoke
Passes their windows, all the brocade seats are full
Eventually out come egg sandwiches and Craven A
No one talks, everyone busy munching, smoking, reading
Strangers sit alone, looking at those opposite, saying nothing
Some hide behind *The Times* or gaze out through dirty windows

Tickets please, most fumble forgetting where they put them
Having found them, they return them to places they forget
Some fall asleep to pass the time, periodically, checking their watches
Warm, smoke hazy, carriages are conducive to sleep, that together with
The chuggity chug chuggity chug regular rhythm of wheels of steel
They drop into a dream till a friendly hand wakes them
'Wake up old chap .We're in London.'

8   The Afghanistan Gong

The Afghanistan gong is a medal
Proof you have served in the campaign
Most volunteers that go there
Have no fear of what might occur
Death and injury are part of the risk

Men and women keen to take
On the challenge, aware but not frightened
United in the task ahead
Not for the money or the glory
Though their loved ones are proud

Excited as they touch down
In a land so far from home
Children smile and welcome them
Old men who have seen it all before
Sit at the roadside and stare, confused and
Annoyed, as if saying leave us alone

Their eyes say it all. Go back home you
Young people. You cannot win here
Many like you have tried before, and failed
Go back home where you belong
Don't exchange your life
For the Afghanistan Gong

9   The Light of Love

I hear that you're going to heaven
Being older I thought I was before you
How come you're going before me?
I bet you are jumping the queue

When you get there tell him I'm coming
Though I can't say when it will be
It might be any day – who knows
It's all written in my destiny

In his house there are many mansions
Better prospects than here no doubt
A single room bungalow will suit me
Near the shops as I suffer with gout

Does God know you are going to heaven?
Have you booked a place through his son
And lived the life of a Christian while
Making sure his commandments are done

Have you been to church every Sunday?
Given money to the sick and the poor
Respected the religions of others?
If you have then one can't ask for more.

Goodbye my dear friend I shall miss you
Your jokes and laughs will be gone
I know I have others to take your place
But from you the light of love shone

10   The Tale of Billy Bong

In the days of years gone by
Billy Bong was young and shy
He didn't smile he just looked sad
Despite kind words from Mum and Dad

Nothing seemed to make him grin
Like slipping on a banana skin
Funny faces he just ignored
He just looked at them very bored

Clowns just did not change his face
His lips were fixed and stayed in place
He seemed to think nothing was funny
Even the antics of his pet rabbit Bunny

Mrs Bong not knowing what to do
Decided to take him to the zoo
He walked around looking very glum
Holding hands with his dad and mum

A woman suddenly gave a shriek of terror
She raised her skirts and not by error
The reason it seems was the sight of a mouse
At this Billy's laughter brought down the house

He shrieked with laughter and curled up with glee
The funny side of the scene he was the first to see
Those stood watching were affected by Billy
They all started laughing, though they felt very silly

Soon the zookeeper was chuckling too
It was the biggest attraction that day in the zoo
I'm pleased to report that by God's good grace
Today you can't take the smile off of Billy's face

11   A Tribute to Elsie

As I stood in the porch outside the Crem
Many floral tributes did I see
Garlands of flowers for all the diseased
Except Elsie
She has just one rose beside her name
It looks so alone and forlorn
The card on it read, 'To Mum
From your loving and only son Shaun.'

A great big lump came into my throat
When I saw all the flowers around
I jumped in my car, and motored to town
Till a flower shop I found
I bought a large bunch of carnations;
The little card with it came free.
I scattered the flowers around her name
As a tribute to poor Elsie

12   The Teas Maid

Doctor gave me some tablets to help me to sleep
Just like a baby and not make a peep

Some time after midnight each night I would wake
And curse it was hours before daylight would break

I would lie in bed just thinking – not dreaming
Of nothing important, of thoughts with no meaning.

So downstairs I'd creep while still it was dark
I had no ambitions to be up with the lark

I would settle down in my favourite armchair
For sleep to over come me I would offer a prayer

I could hear my beloved snoring softly upstairs
Contentedly snoozing as if she hadn't a care

I don't know what time sleep came over me
What woke me was her yelling downstairs

'Make the tea'

13 The Chippy

The greatest joy to pass my lips
Every day is fish and chips
Batter crisp, chips nice and brown
I have tried the best in town.

Cod, it is my choice of fish
Nice large portion on a dish
Tartar is my favourite sauce
Plus salt and vinegar of course

As a boy our chippy would cater
For fish 'n' chips in old newspaper
Restaurants full of heads of grey
Young ones go for take away

Fat and healthy –I thank God
Mostly due to chips and cod
Greasy food we should not eat
It's not good for heart or feet

Some think doctors are pathetic
Eat fish and chips though diabetic
Dad, who died at ninety-one
Had fish and chips inside his tum

If cod and chips do not you please
Have an omelette made with cheese.
If you do not want the latter
Try a sausage fried in batter

14   The Dog Fight

Dozing in the morning sunshine
War is on, and we must fight
At the moment all is quiet
Nerves are taunt, adrenalin high

One eye open, waiting for it
Any moment it will come
Jangling bell, they are approaching
Time again to beat Drake's drum

Grab our jackets, and race to the aircraft
Chocks away, propellers spun
Pick up speed along the tarmac
As we race upwards towards the sun

Tally ho! They're down below us
Now we'll make the blighters pay
Break formation, and find a target
The one ahead will make my day

Throttle open, guns are ready
Listen to the engine whine
I have the fighter in my sights now
Enemy fighter, you are mine

Check my sights, then press the trigger
Rat-a-tat I spit the lead
Plane in tatters, engines burning
Pilot ejects, so he's not dead

Search around to find another
'Behind you John,' I hear Skip say
Glance in mirror, it's coming for me
Dive and spin, and really pray

He clings on, I cannot shake him
I fear my life about to end
Suddenly, I see him pass me
Skipper got him – what a friend

Skirmish over, head for home now
Shot up fuselage to mend
Enemy now in disarray
They'll be back you can depend

Gratefully we land on airstrip
Every day just like the rest
Except today we lost no buddies
Yesterday, we lost the best

15   The Last of the Company

Rows of medals adorned the soldier's breast
From wars fought all over the world
Each one a bitter memory of friends he had lost
When he thought of them his upper lip curled

Aged seventeen he took the King's shilling
Which he spent on Woodbines and beer
Initiation into war was at the Battle of Somme
Where he learnt to overcome fear

Shells rained down on them every day
The weather filled their trenches with rain
He could still feel a lump of shrapnel in his leg
But he could never get rid of the pain

He got a Victoria Cross for his gallantry
Just by accident it seemed at the time
When single-handed he managed to capture
A company of a hundred and nine

It wasn't all doom and gloom in those days
He had lots of fun as well in the war
Once he played football with the enemy
And a goal he managed to score

At ninety he's the last one left of his company
As he marches past the Cenotaph, he recalls
Captain Smith, Private Snoops and Corporal Tarter
Each one, though dead, can walk tall

16   The Rules of Teaching

I remember when I was at school
Teacher used to hit me with a rule
I was always the one she picked on
Just for playing the fool

I was a bit noisy in the school yard
To that fact I have to confess
Though cowboys isn't a quiet game
But she referred to me as a pest

It's not fair I always got the blame
The girls would snitch on me
For trying to cadge a kiss or a sweet
Behind the old boys lavatory

I was often sent home from school
With a note explaining to mum
Just why I had been suspended
She'd give me a smack on my bum

My homework was always a mess
It interfered with going to play
She wouldn't accept my excuses
And said with the rules I would pay

I am an old man myself now
Things are so different in school
Kids are the same, the punishments changed
Teachers can't hit kids with a rule

17   Memories Slipping

I have just lost a very good friend of mine
His loss has caused me much sorrow
I stood alone at the churchyard waiting
Then I realised the funerals tomorrow

I felt such a fool when I came home to tea
Wife said 'Well, how did the funeral go?'
I didn't like to tell her I'd stood there alone
Like a fool, in the frost and the snow

I said 'Funeral! What funeral? You mean Bert's?'
She said 'Yes.' 'It's not till tomorrow,' I said
'That's strange because I saw Bert's cortege pass by
He's being cremated instead.'

18   The Mother of the Mendips

Wells Cathedral is the Queen of the Mendips
Her home is the City of Wells which
Is the smallest city in England, I'm told
Her subjects are its citizens
Her courtiers are the people of the world

They visit, and marvel at her ancient beauty
She sits majestically at the foot of these hills
Guarded by triple tall towers who support
Her ample, spacious nave, and hold the bells
Which ring forth both glad tidings, in court

Her robes, which she has worn for hundreds
Of years, are bedecked in a multitude
Of statues of kings, bishops and apostles
And yet, she remains spotlessly, gleaming clean
As she smiles down on the multitudes

Large, well-cut lawns surround her feet
Like a green carpet,her subjects of all nations
Begrudge no time, or money, to her upkeep
She has on her left tower, a large clock;
Where two knights of old, strike bells telling the time
Silent witnesses, to countless years gone by
Visitors who paint, or take her photograph in admiration

On entering, via one of its many doors, one cannot fail
To sense the cool, serene, quietness of its interior
 Conversations spoken in whispers, in reverence to what
After all, is the house of God
Soft music from its massive organ; permeates around
The high balconies, and every nook and cranny
So all within may hear its dulcet sounds

The flagstones of the nave worn by millions of souls
Who have scuffed over them
Illegible grave stones are dotted over its surface
Like untidy discarded playing cards
Plaques of love ones, long departed, adorn the walls
A gathering of tourists stare wondrously, and patiently
Waiting to see, the oldest clock in the world,
Strike the current hour, of its twenty-four
Just as it has done for seven hundred years
Knights on horseback chase each other until one is unseated
The Queen holds so many treasures in her breasts
Like Jack Blandiver; whose past is unknown
He keeps a wary eye on the millions he has seen
May this mighty cathedral; last another thousand years
Until the Mendip hills become flat plains
And time with us is no more

19   The Waiting Room

I look around the room that I'm in
So silent one could hear a dropped pin
They all sit there waiting patiently
By appointment for their doctor to see

There's a man with a hacking cough
On whose chest he can't get it off
There's a young lady smartly dressed
Wants the doctor to examine her chest

A young scruffy lad with rings in his nose
Wants another week off work I suppose
Another man has one arm in a sling
On his knee a little boy clings

I wonder what's wrong with her over there
She's got spotty skin, and light brown hair
There's a man reading an old magazine
Has the biggest nose that I've ever seen

An old lady sits with her Zimmer frame
No body can see, but she's in great pain
Next to me sits a pregnant mum
With a great big swelling in her tum

Suddenly the buzzer rings for me
I've waited all of ten minutes you see
It's cold outside, its mid December
What have I come for? I can't remember

20   Somerset Poacher

I been a poacher more than sixty years
So was my father and granddad before
They trained me, and taught me all I know
To take just what we needed; and no more

At the dead of night I would set my traps
Being careful to avoid the keeper
Rabbits were on sale in the market place
But my way, they were a lot cheaper

I was caught once when I was a boy
By the gamekeeper of the estate
He grabbed me as I was sneaking past
A broken down five bar gate

He boxed my ears till my head spun
I was annoyed, after all I'd been taught
'It wasn't for trespassing,' he said
But it was for getting caught

The poaching today is for big game
Like the big stags on the Quantocks
Or the salmon that leaps in the Spey
Big punishments come as shock

So I've hung up my gin traps and snares
What I learnt in the past, I've forgotten
The sense of fun we used to have then
Has died in my memory, and is rotten

21   The Son in Law

If you want a son in law
First you have to have a daughter
Your daughter's choice may not
Be yours, so what?

She has vowed to be his wife
It's something you can't alter
Now you have a man about
Who is not exactly kith and kin
It's the girl he fell in love with not you

If you want to get along with him
Treat him like a man, better still
Treat him like a son
Love him and respect him
And soon you will find
His affection you have won

You have found a son
A good one will always be
There to help you, and advice
Just like your real son, in his eyes

22   Bloody Hard Times

Empty pockets, count the pennies
Check my wallet, no money there
Need the bus fare for the children
And the larders looking bare

Can just afford this week's rent
Car must stay untaxed again
Child allowance due tomorrow
Keeping family life sustained

What's all this about the euro?
Has it owt to do with us?
I couldn't spend it if I had one
Don't see why there's all this fuss

Christmas is three weeks off now
I been saving very hard
Buying things down at Argos
Mostly on my credit card

Bought our Johnny a computer
And our Sal a mobile phone
Nearly four hundred quid's worth
And I bet they both still moan

Bert's been out of work all week
Oxfam jacket looks like rags
In and out the pubs and bookies
Seeing if he can scrounge some fags

When will things start to get better?
That's what we all want to know
Coalition? What a mock-up
Just enough money for tonight's Bingo

23   The Caravan Club

How I wish I had stayed in the caravan club
Where I could roam where ever I pleased
With my Ford Mondeo hitched up to the van
And the knob on my bumper well greased

I enjoyed caravanning over in Wales;
It's so much more peaceful than here.
Lots of green hills, and chuckling streams
Plenty of places to stop for a beer

We had lots of mates in the caravan club
Who we were always eager to see
They would help us unhitch, and get set up
Then invite us round, for biscuits and tea

It was fun to tour in a new area
See sights we'd before never seen.
It was a nuisance having to fetch water
And to continually empty the latrine

Despite all those annoying setbacks
I only have one thing to say.
We finished our life of caravanning
And sold the old van on ebay

24   The Airport

Approach the airport carefully, traffic very heavy
Parking very difficult, infringement a big levy
Unload baggage from the cab, go and find a trolley
Drivers waving furiously, forgot to pay him lolly

Walking into airport, thousands do the same
Look to find departure board, then to find my plane
Must look after baggage, cannot leave unattended
I must keep it with me or police will be offended

Check in desk staff very good, speedy and polite
Baggage weighed and labelled -30K, just right
I feel I can relax now, and look around the shops
Buy Mum a little present and Dad a bottle of scotch

Two hours yet till take-off, I decide to have a doze
Having very happy dream – till a fly lands on my nose
This makes me wake up instantly, I check my watch again
Not only have I overslept, I've gone and missed my plane

25   The Sunday Roast

My favourite meal and to which I give this toast
Is that succulent, savoury, satisfying Sunday roast
When times were hard and meat was on the ration
The Sunday roast was still very much in fashion

Mum bought the best joint she could afford
With roast she knew we would never be bored
Very often the little joint had to last the week
First roast, then cold, then mince with leeks

The smell it was scrumptious, it permeated each room
Roasting in the enamel pan, deep in the oven gloom
Basting it every so often, to keep it moist and lean
Vegetables boiling away, filling the house with steam

Roast potatoes, and Yorkshires were all part of the meal
Fresh veg from the garden, made the meal taste real
When the meat was ready, and the family all sat down
Dad would take charge, and slice the meat, juicy and brown

Dark juices from the meat ran on to the carving plate
We all watch eagerly, no one was ever late
Mother had made the gravy, thick, brown and tasty
Sunday roast took a lot of time, one just couldn't be hasty

Nobody missed the Sunday roast; we ate every bit
If some one suggested an alternative mum would have a fit
Beef, pork, then roast lamb; no chicken, or turkey you see
In the days when I was a lad, they were classed as luxuries

26   The Village Dentist

I am the local dentist; a toothache I can cure
I greet them with a smile as they come in the door
I have a little surgery located on the street
Cautiously they enter, many with cold feet

My surgery is spotless, pretty pictures on the wall
Most come by appointment, some don't come at all
I make them feel at home, as I sit them in my chair
And when I tilt it back, it's up their nose I stare

Straight away I start, with my mirror and my probe
My assistant's there to help me, dressed in her white robe
I look down at my patient; her eyes are squeezed up tight
Sweat is showing on her brow, she really is a sight

I try to relax her, but her hands are clamped to the chair
I would suggest a filling, but I don't know if I dare
I just start up my drill, to do that filling that I saw
When with a shriek she jumps up, and rushes for the door

A lovely lady came one day she said she was in pain
I looked, and said I'd take it out, her face began to drain
She says she would rather have a baby and fixed me with a glare
I said to her 'make up your mind, before I adjust the chair'

27   The Plastic Cup

I take my shoes off and stand on the wet sand where
Seconds before the sea had lightly kissed before retreating
Each of my feet clearly imprinted for just a moment
Before being erased by another ripple of the gentle incoming tide

The sea is blue and tranquil as far as the eye can see
No white horses are galloping to pound and bully the shore
White sails in the distant struggle to find some breeze
The air is fragrant and still, recovering from yesterday's storm

The warm summer sun would melt butter, I am happy until
I see a white plastic cup carelessly discarded lolling backwards
And forwards, as each fresh tide makes its progress shorewards
I am suddenly aware that this intruder will be like driftwood
And seaweed, and become beach litter

I bend and pick it up feeling annoyed that this piece
Of rubbish should be allowed to spoil such a tranquil scene
Gently kicking water I stroll along the beach going nowhere special
Today is magnificent; it is as rare as a diamond in a dustbin
I gaze upwards towards the cloudless sky, and pray for more
Of the same tomorrow

28   The Pensioner's Lament

A pensioner sat upon a bench
His head was bent very low
I went and sat down next to him
If he saw me, it didn't show

I talked about the weather
He seemed reluctant to chat
When I mentioned holidays
His old face really fell flat

'A holiday?' he said, with a grunt
'I've no money for things like that.'
'You have pensions haven't you?'
When I said it his face fell flat

'Don't talk about pensions
I got done out of mine
Forty years I worked for them
I thought my pension was fine

'The firm had squandered the lot
I had been paying in all my life
I get a bit from the State I know
But I've got to support my wife.'

I really did feel sorry for him.
Then it suddenly started to rain
I said goodbye, ran to my Rolls
And flew off to my villa in Spain

29   The Old Radio

On the shelf in a old junk shop
Sat a radio all on its own
Not only did the old radio work
But it had a very good tone

Its brown veneered case was dusty
It was cracked and worn with age
One of its knobs was broken
All three were the colour of beige

No body wanted to buy it now
To clean it up would be a chore
But what everyone seems to forget
It announced the Second World War

It recited the wise words of Churchill
General De Gaulle and Roosevelt too
Songs by Bing and Shirley Temple
To mention just a few

Mind you, it needed a big battery
An accumulator cost a few pennies
What it didn't need was electricity
Just as well as there wasn't any

30   The State of the Roads

Oh when are they going to mend the roads?
They're getting all pitted and bumpy

I went and complained to the council
But they weren't helpful, just grumpy

There are holes so big if you fell in them
You would never be seen again

There's a big one just across the road,
And a bigger one down Strawberry Lane

My old car she rattles enough
On a road that's smooth and true

But after driving on these roads
The metal on my tyres come through

Something just has to be done
After all the road tax we pay

I have a good mind to write to my MP
But he's never here, he's always away

31   The Empty Castle

The climb to the castle is very steep
Very weary we approach the gates
Tall forbidding bastions peered down on us
With battlements dressed in ivy
Crows spiral above us like snarling Spitfires
They seem to say 'Go away'
It looks as if it wants to be left alone

It does not welcome strangers
A spiral stone staircase takes us to the roof
The wonderful view obstructed by scaffolding
Trying to preserve another crumbling fortification
Fighting a loosing battle
Like those who defended her years ago

Dark damp rooms, bare of living essentials
Wallpaper, a job lot, torn, tattered and faded
All the rooms are stripped bare
Unwelcome visitors stand and stare, bemused
Satisfied, but mystified. Why do they come?
There's nothing to see, only history

32   The Magpie

Another day and you are here again
Can I assume you are the same one as yesterday?

You are the most arrogant and brash bully
Yet I salute you, for fear you are just one in number
'One for sorrow,' as they say

You have a reputation as a thief, is that true?
Rossini knew you so very well
He even wrote an overture titled 'The Thieving Magpie'

You are unmistakeable in your piebald evening dress
With its long tail. You are the Fred Astaire of bird land
As you foxtrot daintily along my garden fence

Have you changed? I doubt it
I hear you in the firs, taking charge
Not adverse to the odd egg, or chick
Unloved even by your own kind

You are a bad example; go away and mend your ways
Till then you are not welcome in my garden
No wait, don't go. You add some colour to my
Garden in this drab winter period. Come back
But next time bring a friend

33 Pack It In

We are going camping, me and my husband Jack
I've never been camping before so I don't know what to pack
I'll start with his long johns; 'cos it might get cold at night
And a pretty nighty for me that I can tie up really tight

I must pack his pyjamas; he likes the striped ones with the cord
I got them at the jumble sale it was all I could afford
I better take a nice dress, in case we go out for dinner
Next time will be the first, he's as tight as a drummer's skinner

Now what shoes shall I take? I think eight pairs is enough?
I can always buy more if the weather gets rough
I like to wear stiletto best, as I am rather short
And I'll pack his running shoes; as he likes his bit of sport

Now where has he left his slippers? they're not under the bed
I bet he's gone and hid them so I'll take his new ones instead
He's bound to need some ties; I think I'll take these three
Ah his rolled neck sweater with a badge on, that will pack easy

I better pack a suit for him, in case we go to church
First time was when we got married, and he left me in the lurch
Ah there's his blazer, and grey flannels too
I like my man to look smart, now, what next must I do?

I'll need my bikini, coloured chocolate brown
It fitted twenty years ago, but I've put on a couple of pounds
Of course he'll need his shorts; I better pack six pairs
Another pair of shoes for him, he left under the stairs

Now what about some wellies, it's bound to pour with rain
And our macs will do another year, I better make that plain
There, I think that's just about the lot. I've filled six cases already
Let's see, oh yes I nearly forgot. I better take his teddy

34   Sailor Boy

Jack the lad was a sailor boy
Who went sailing with his dad
His dad said that Jack was
The best crew he had ever had

They sailed in a big sailing ship
Across the seven stormy seas
They traded in what ever they could
Whether meat or tea or cheese

Sometimes the seas were very
Rough with waves as big as a house
But Jack carried out his duties
Efficiently and as quiet as a mouse

One day a great big wave came in
And broke the ship's mast in two
Jack's dad was very concerned,
And said 'Whatever shall we do?'

I know said Jack to his dad
There is wreck upon the sand
It has got a lovely mast
On our ship it would look grand

So Dad and crew went and got it
And fitted it to their boat
It only took a day or two
And they were soon afloat

'Eh lad,' said Dad, 'you are the best
I have in all my crew
Keep on sailing on the sea
A ship's captain you will be too.'

35   The Unlucky Black Cat

Introductory note

My previous wife and I lost two children: my daughter, Shelagh Marie, who died unexpectedly in her mother's arms aged five months and my only son Phillip John who came home from boarding school and fell inside a hollow willow tree strangling himself in the branches.

Wedding photo showing the black cat shooting out of the window.

Black cats are suppose to be lucky
Though a sad little story I tell
Of a boy and a girl who got married
And on whom good luck did rebel

The service was a great success
And the photos were clear and bright
So off to the reception they all went
To indulge in the food with delight

Just as they were about to cut the cake
The black cat thought to take its leave
Their good fortune it would take
Away with no hint of how much they'd grieve

A black cat entering a room I agree
Is a sign that everything's well
But to find one doing an exit
Tells of gloom, of which I must tell

Everything went well for a year or two
They thought their marriage was charmed
Then their baby girl of five months old
Died unexpectedly in her mother's arms

She was the youngest child of the three
It left one small pretty girl and a boy
The parents were naturally very upset
Baby Shelagh was their pride and joy

The following years went by without a hitch
The boy went to a boarding school for free
He came home on holiday twelve years old
When he accidentally strangled himself in a tree

Just after that the marriage broke up
They each went their own separate ways
They both never forgot their two children
Until the day they both went to their graves

36   No Space for Women

The rush for men to get into Space
Left American girls out of the race
Housewives, girlfriends and mothers
They could be, but a real astronaut
Was born don't you see? Not taught

This was all very well for a little while
But later the women really got riled
They said they could do it, just as well
If the answer was no, to Congress they'd yell

The pressure on NASA to great to oppose
After the Russians to the challenge rose
Sent up Valentina Tereshkova all alone
Next into space, the first American girl rode

The name of the woman was Sally Ride
About time too, the women all cried
It made quite a change to replace a man
The second to fly was Kath Sullivan

Not only was she the third girl in the race
She was the first woman to walk in space
The men by now were used to all this
Accepted women were not there just to kiss

The first black girl was Mae Jemison
Who taught the men some new lessons
Miss Sharman the first Brit in space to fly
Was paid for by Russian generosity

We cannot forget Christina Mc Aucliffe
The first women to die on *Challenger*'s lift
How many more must we lose in this race?
To prove we need women as well as men in space

37 Silence

One cannot appreciate silence until
One stands in a field of death
Like a military cemetery
Each gravestone naming the hero it is there for
They were witness to their comrade's death, and their own
No birds sing
No vehicles thunder by
No aeroplanes in the sky
Just silence

Now white rounded gravestones
Uniform in straight lines, still at attention
As if on the parade ground of death
Rows of flowers adorn these immaculate graves
But even here
No birds sing.
No vehicles thunder by
No aeroplanes in the sky
Just silence

Stand in the cemetery at Bergen Belsen
Surrounded by tall fir trees
Many huge mounds of grass-covered earth
With plaques announcing
'Five thousand buried here'
Victims of the Final Solution
No birds sing
No vehicles thunder by
No aeroplanes in the sky
Just silence

38   The Ozone Layer

The ozone layer is part of the atmosphere
Where a hole has just suddenly appeared
We are concerned that the world might change
Desserts appear where once there was rain
Wet stormy winters and hot summer days
Storms and flooding and scorching sun rays

Ice caps are melting that we all know
Already we find there is very little snow
When this will happen we are not really sure
Though sunny days we can certainly endure
Great Britain, bless it, is doing its best
Though not China, India and most of the rest

Are we trying to achieve what nature can't do?
Have we bitten off more than we can chew?
Is this just another stage of evolution?
Like changes to which there is no solution
There are things in life we can do nothing about
Like one day when the sun's light goes out

39   The Pheasant

Pheasants are a silly bird
Usually very slow and fat
I bet you've never seen a clever one
You must admit to that
Oh they are very pretty
Their plumage quite divine
But they are only bred for eating
And to me, well that's just fine

If one should see you coming
As you drive along the lanes
It sort of stands and watches you
Its intentions never plain
Just as you are about to pass it
She decides it's time to cross
Expecting you to stop dead
Because she is the boss

I know they cannot fly far
Their wings aren't made for that
But if you should ever roast one
Cover its breast in bacon fat
Now where was I?
Ah yes, this funny bird
Reminds me of the Dodo
Pretty, but absurd

There are roads quite near here
Where if you're walking you will find
The road carpeted with dead ones
Squashed flat I recall to mind
Killed by motorists who cannot wait
To let the old birds pass
Have to belt them with their mudguards
Right up their tiny bottoms

40   Scutari Hospital (Crimea)

Gently and tenderly she trod between rows of frozen toes
Her shoes encased with their shit; mixed with the blood of dying men
To whom she was only permitted to offer a prayer, and a smile
She could hear the screams of amputation
Carried out without anaesthetic

Brave men, poorly clad, ill equipped for winter condition
Besides herself and a few other females, no body cared
At home; apart from loved ones, no body cared
They were written off as cannon fodder
The ladies could look, sympathise and watch brave men die
They were forbidden to help
Though that was their reason for being there

No beds
No blankets
No cooking utensils
No bandages,
No medical supplies
No anything
Plenty of beer and port, hardly the ammunition to fight a war on
The nurses fared as bad as the men
Had one pan each to do everything in-nothing else
Hundred of wounded men arriving each week to die
The forgotten heroes of Scutari

41   Yesterday's Lover

You entered my dreams again last night
Why can't you keep away, yesterday's lover
You have no place in my heart now
Only memories, even those are fading fast

You who I once loved so dearly
Who I would have done anything for
Yet you used me, played with my affections
Paying them off with false promises

You knew you would never come to me
Although I begged you
I was your plaything to be enjoyed
Then discarded like a rag doll until
You needed me once more

In desperation and frustration
I found the strength to go my own way
Find a new and trustworthy love
But you would not let me go. Oh no
You asked me to be untrue to my new bride

I have kept my marital vows
My wife is all I could wish for
We will stay together till our last breath
You are lonely now and well deserved
I have happiness. Please don't come back

42   The Prawn and the Lobster

A lobster came upon a prawn one day
He said 'I'm having you for my dinner.'
The prawn was about to scuttle away
Compared to the crab he was slimmer

Mr Lobster was getting old and frail
His legs had gone wobbly and thin
Mr Hole the Dover sole said scathingly
'I think you should be in a tin.'

Mr Lobster caught the prawn in his claw
'Wait Mr Lobster, don't eat me, I plead.'
The lobster was about to open his jaw
'For one day my services you might need.'

He thought about it and let the prawn go
The prawn felt so good to be free
Poor Mr Lobster still had a problem
What would he be having for tea?

He came across an old black lobster pot
And thought he would look inside
He climbed up the side and fell in the hole
He was trapped. 'Help! Help!' he cried

No one was near to help him out
He knew he could die there alone
It was then he realised what he'd done
He had left his mobile at home

It was then that Mr Prawn passed by
'Can I help Mr Lobster?' he enquired
'Oh yes please,' begged Mr Lobster in tears
'I feel my life in here will expire.'

'It would Mr Lobster I feel sure of that,
You would die in this pot there's no doubt
I will see what I can do to set you free.'
And with that he pulled the locking pin out

'I'm free, I'm free,' shouted Mr Lobster
'Mr Prawn you are a real winner
I solemnly promise from this day forth
I will never eat a prawn for my dinner.'

43   Helping Out

When I was just a little lad
And money was hard to get too
I did what I could to help out
Though there wasn't a lot I could do

I would take my bike to the station
Approach folks with cases quite heavy
Put their case on my bike, and walk with them
And charge them a sixpenny levee

I would go up the woods and pick hazel nuts
They were wild, and growing free
I would take them home and bag them up
Sell them a bag for ten pee

We had an old apple tree in the garden
The fruit from it not very good
The coach people were happy to buy them off me
So I sold as many as I could

I would stand around our cathedral
And offer myself as a guide
I didn't know one end from the other
But you had to admit that I tried

Dad was away fighting a war
Money was in short supply
By my helping out, it eased the strain
And a few extras mum was able to buy

44   The Lady and Her Kitten

The lady lies on the sofa asleep
On her lap is the cat she adores
It settles down making no noise
It stretches out exposing its claws

Together they lay and they dream
The lady of love, the cat of cream
The lady dreams of wonderful things
The cat of a trout in a nearby stream

The cat lies in front of the fire
Food, warmth and friendship is all it needs
The lady is lonely, she yearns for love
A phone call from Basra, she pleads

Her soldier boy has been away a year
He has phoned, and he has written
But she needs his loving arms around her
Till then she will love his kitten

45 Sainsbury's

'Mummy,' said Sophie 'Can we go for a walk?'
Kate said, 'I would prefer to stay in and chalk.'
'We're going to Sainsbury's, so get in the car.'
'Let's walk it ,' says Sophie. 'It's not very far.'

'Alright,' says Mummy, 'that's what we'll do
Kate, remember to tie up your shoe.'
'Can I take my scooter?' Sophie enquired
'I'll take my dolls pram ,' said Kate, looking tired

The shopping complete they met Nanny there too
'I thought that you had a day at the zoo.'
'No not today, Nanny, we had to come here.'
Just then 'Stop thief' was heard from the rear

A man came running with a bag in his fist
Nearly knocked Nanny over and only just missed
Sophie pushed her scooter right into his toes
He tripped and went flying, and let the bag go

The bag flew through the air into Kate's pram
The doorman came running whose name was Sam
'Where is the bag or am I too late?'
The thief knew that Jail was his only Fate

'I got the bag here,' said Kate with a smile
'Well done, young lady. You're slick by a mile.'
Sophie said, 'I pushed the scooter into his way.'
'Well done, young lady what more can I say.'

The manager came and said, 'What's this I hear?
These two young ladies have shown no fear
I'm so impressed that a reward I must pay
Choose from our shop what you fancy today.'

The press were there in less than five mins
By golly, thought Nanny, they're quick on their pins
The manager said, 'My car's waiting to take you all home
If we can be of service don't hesitate to phone.'

Sophie and Kate both had rewards galore
It seemed they were going to empty the store
Just as the car drove them away in the rain
Sophie said, 'That was fun, can we do it again?'

46   The Sons of Vimey Ridge

It's Easter Monday. 1917. We are
Defending Vimey in France
Canadian forces in the distance
Prepare us for their next advance
Shells have landed all around us
I am weary – aren't we all?
'Come on lads we can beat them.'
Is our platoon sergeant's call

Rain-filled trenches we are used to
I forget when I felt dry
Belly's like an empty cupboard
Maybe better if I die
My friend Schultz has lost a brother
It all seems a waste of time
Haven't gained a foot of ground yet
I can hear the bullets whine

'Listen! I can hear them coming.'
Whispered orders meant to cheer
Clink of metal in the distance
Still I can't absorb the fear
Through tear-filled eyes I spy their leader
Young lieutenant fresh from home
Webley pistol against my Mauser
What chance has he with that silly gun?

Rat-a-tat, they fall like ninepins
Subaltern is first to die
They're determined to take us this time
Dead bodies in the trenches lie
To retreat is not a choice
Barbed wire slows down their progress
Still they come with fearsome voice

Now they're jumping in our trenches
It's hand to hand with knife and gun
Bloodcurdling yells from a Scotsman
As his long bayonet in me runs
My eyes are closed with heavy lids
Our German forces are surrendering
I know that my life is ending
Defeated sons of Vimey Ridge

47   Welcome to Weston-super-Mare

People come to Weston
For sun, good food, and fun
To meet the folks of Somerset
From where best cider comes
To walk along the promenade
Venture on our brand new pier
Everyone is welcome
Every day of the year

We sell every kind of food here
From countries far and wide
There's loads of fish and chip shops
And you can paddle in the tide
We even have a revolving eye
Folks love to have a go
It only costs a few pounds
And it does go very slow

We have the biggest collection
Of helicopters in the land
Not only can you get inside them
But flights are in demand
When you've finished flying
There's lots more one can do
We have a good Aquarium
But we haven't got a zoo (not yet)

The sea it comes in twice a day
As regular as clockwork
Have a win on the slot machines
That's another perk
We have the Sovereign Centre
Where bargains can be had
It's an ideal place to go
If the weather should turn bad.

Then there are the Winter Gardens
And Playhouse Theatre too
Rumours that they're pulling down
The Tropicana and making it a Zoo
Our councillors are not bad
Their life it is not all honey
I think they have made Weston
Beautiful, on very little money

48   The Fisherman's Dream

The fisherman sat on the river bank
His line in the water was still
His mind was not on what he was doing
It was on his sick wife Jill

A tear rolled down his weathered face
He wiped it on his sleeve
Nobody else was fishing that day
No one to witness his grief

He saw the movement on his float
His reaction was automatic
He flicked his rod sharply to the right
The response was hardly pathetic

He forgot about his sick wife Jill
As his line tore off down the stream
He played it very carefully
This was truly a fisherman's dream

It took half an hour to land it
An eight pound carp he had there
He would have taken it home to Jill
But realised it really wasn't fair

So he put the fish back in the water
When his mobile rang to say
That while he had been fishing
His wife Jill had passed away

49   Billy the Boxer

Old Billy had been a boxer
But he hadn't boxed for years
He sported a big fat broken nose
And a pair of cauliflower ears

His brain is now all fuzzy
And his eyes are very dim
But when he was a boxer
He could take it on the chin

His hearing isn't up to much
And he has an awful cough
He'd get back in the ring today
If the purse was big enough

He runs a boys' boxing club
A credit to the boxing man
He used to box in fairgrounds
That's where his training began

Billy, he is boxing no more
He's passed to the grand ring above
He won't be wearing angel's wings
Just boxing shorts and his gloves

50　Christmas 2012

Hey man get with it, it's Christmas tomorrow
If I run out of cash though, more credit I borrow
There's a party tonight we'll get drunk till we're blind
Watch for the coppers, but our parents don't mind

On the computer I send out my Christmas cards
Or text them on my mobile, it's not very hard
I'm quite happy to get them that way, and hey
My bird's having our first baby on Christmas day

These carols and trimmings are a bit of a pain
Though I do like getting presents, let's make that plain
Mince pies and Christmas cake don't pass my lips
I am quite satisfied with a meal of pizza and chips

Mum is divorced, so things now aren't the same
It used to be fun, when Dad played the game
I would normally be out with my mates on Christmas Day
This time it will be at the hospital, with my baby I pray

Christmases in the past I've tried not to take part
With all the palaver of presents and cards
I've been quite content to do my own thing
Ignoring Christian joviality this festive time brings

Times have changed now I'm happy to say
I have a wife, and a child, and one on the way
We decorate and celebrate like all Christians do
It's the birthday of Jesus we raise our glass too

51   Blind Date

I was in between marriages, as one might say
Enjoying life, at work and at play
Weekends and evenings I was at my best
Plenty of friends, I was glad when I rest

Five years of fun I managed to pack in
I was a freeman, committing no sin
But as time passed by, a thought came from above
That what I needed was some one to love

Many girls I had met, but had fallen for none
I was continually searching for the right one
A friend said she had found the right girl for me
It was a blind date, and her name was Jinty

Her cooking was wonderful, she knew how to please
She dressed like a film star, and loved eating Chinese
As she was a teacher she gave me some tests
I failed at maths, but did biology best

She is the boss, there is no doubt on that score
The pleasure she gives me, no man could ask more
Although it was a blind date, I'm glad to find
She's exactly the girl that I had in mind

52   The Fisherman's Double Whammy

The day is warm and sunny and I am fishing
On the river bank, all alone. Nothing is happening
My mobile rings

At the same time my float dives under the water
And the line screams from my reel
I grab the rod. I need two hands to handle this fish
The rod tip is bent nearly double

The fish is fighting like a trapped tiger
And I am scared I might lose it
Gently I play it, taking in a little line each time
It seems to take ages, in reality its minutes

Eventually I draw it in and recover in my landing net
It is a big carp; the biggest I have ever caught
Taking the hook out of its mouth I weigh it

It scales at eight pounds. I am a very happy fisherman
It's then I remember the now silent mobile
I pick it up and read the fax
'Grandson born today. Eight pounds'

53 The Ups and Downs of Being a Gentleman

I was taught how to be a gentleman
Good manners are important, you see
I don't mind putting the seat down for ladies
If only they'd lift it up for me

54   The Fishing Boat

The fishing boat sails
In the foggy, cold North Sea
Catching fish for us
Will he succeed? Wait and see
Because some never come home

55   The Reply to a Marriage Proposal

This is a reply to the message you sent
Asking me what was my marriage intent

The reply to your letter may come as a blow
But you asked for it, so I will let both barrels go

Well, I have thought it over what you had said
And I know you are wealthy and posh and well bred

Firstly you smell of male perfume
A little I don't mind, but yours fills the room

You think you're God's gift to women in bed
It's only your satisfaction matters in your head

You're never on time, you always are late
That's one trait in a man I really do hate.

You lie just like a cheap Japanese watch
While your breath always smells of duty free scotch.

It's always my money you spend on our dates
And although you have plenty, parting with it you hate

You don't seem to like good friends of mine
And when asked out as a foursome you never have time

You think I love you and find you a joy
When secretly I find you're a real mummy's boy

So thank you my darling for the letter you sent
But marrying you I have no intent

56 The Yanks Are Coming

In 1943 when the Yanks came over
We thought they lived in a field of clover
Loaded with money, smart uniforms too
Our poor lads didn't know what to do

Many of our girls went out with them
Given nylon stockings, complete with hem
All us kids were after their gum
They in return were after our mum

They had food we thought was rationed
Dressed their girls in the latest fashion
Drove their jeeps most everywhere
Oversexed, and over here

One day we woke to find them gone
To fight a war not yet won
They had families like you and me
And had said goodbye to win a victory

57   The Pill Collector

Some people are funny that take pills every day
They seem to like to collect different sorts
Red ones, white ones, all different colours
The more rare the shape, the better the sport

They put you down when you tell them
About the pills the doctor said you must take
'I was on those once,' they will say
'But not now, because they kept me awake.'

It's worse when you see them at mealtimes
They don't quietly take them with a drink
They spread them out like men on parade
One dreads what other diners must think

They are an authority on all that's available
And what each tablet can do
It doesn't matter what the doctor prescribed
They know what's the best one for you

They will even insist you try one of theirs
It will cure your complaint in the end
And if you should die as a result of it
Well, at least it was prescribed by a friend

58   Nicely Proportioned

Blond haircut and styled
With studs in nose, lips and ears
Her eyes of blue and rosy lips
Frame teeth whiter than snow drops
On each shoulder sits a butterfly

Breasts like half grapefruits
Round and firm
Proud nipples fight for air
Separated by a tiny cleavage
Her studded navel bare

Her legs so long and slender
Light tanned by summer sun
On her back a tattooed flower
Small and discreetly placed
Just above the slimline waist

Her hips look made to measure
Add balance to her dainty frame
God made beauty passes by
Blessed with a small flat tum
And denim clad mini curvy bum

59   The Convoy Escort

The year is 1942
Weathers freezing, fingers blue
Convoys moving stealth fully
Guarded by the Kings Navy

U boats prowling in a pack
Eyes alert, meals just a snack
Each man knows just what to do
They are a team, they are the crew

Suddenly, night sky lights up
A mighty bang, thoughts interrupt
Hunter sub has got his prey
It will cost him, he will pay

Sailors jumping in the sea
Jumping into misery
All the sea is thick with oil
Healthy lungs, the sea will spoil

They must be left to their fate
We cannot let this sub escape
Circle wide and drop a pattern
Depth charges will make subs flatten

Silence for a little while, then
Boom-boom-boom, the captain smiles
Have we got it? Goodness knows
Suddenly, an oil slick shows

Loud cheers from the lads on board
A killer sub we have just scored
Hunting killers is no fun
Captain orders tots of rum

Back on duty, alert once more
Must add another to our score
Can't believe it, sub in the sites
It must have surfaced in the night

They've surrendered – one and all
Now home to blighty, have a ball
Hoist the flag as we sail in
Captain deserves a large pink gin.

60   Looking for a Husband

I'm looking for a lover who would like to marry me
I don't mind if he wears glasses as long as he can see

He don't have to be a big bloke with tattoos on his arm
He can be a little skinny runt as long as he has charm

I wouldn't mind if he had one leg and had to walk with a crutch
I would carry on with my day job though the pay's not up to much

I would love to cuddle up to him and blow out the candle in bed
And if he didn't want it we could read to each other instead

I would cook and clean for him just like his mum used to do
When I ask him about other loves I don't mind if he's had a few

I don't mind if we have children or not, perhaps he's too old for that
Content to cuddle up in front of the fire, just me and him and the cat

61   Message from Santa

Santa's not coming this Christmas
He says he has a bad chill
And he complains his back is aching
Carrying big sacks up the hill

He says he broke his glasses
And can't see as well as he could
Rudolph has to show him around
And sometimes ends up in a wood

He moans he's not getting younger
Driving the sledge gives him pain
He really should go to the doctor
His energy is beginning to drain

He hasn't eaten since Sunday
He doesn't want food at all
Wait and see what the doctor says
Because he has promised to call

I asked him what the doctor said
He said 'He told me I should
Sit down and make myself comfortable
And eat a large Christmas pud.'

I said, 'Santa, what about all the children
Who are waiting for you to call?
How can I tell them you're not coming?
It just wouldn't be Christmas at all.'

'Don't you worry, I know what to do
I will be there even though I am ill
And just in case I can't make it
I'll send my twin brother, Phil.'

62 A Lonely Christmas

We are on our own this Christmas
It's just your Nan and me
I can't see us affording a turkey
We shall have sandwiches and tea

I hope we get some Christmas cards
To hang up on our wall
Last year we got sacksful
This year I expect we'll get none at all

It's the first year we've been alone
We really don't know what to do
Whether to go to the Indian in town
Or stay at home and have left over stew

I expect we will get a few presents
Grandchildren never forget us
They know we can't get about these days
Though at the end of the road is the bus

In the evening we will sit watching telly
Just like we have done for years
We'll toast you all with a glass of port
And maybe a couple of beers

Don't worry about us, go and have fun
We'll be here when you get back
Remember the laughs when you were young
It was all fun and never a smack.

I expect something will turn up soon
It's only the first of December
We're just feeling a bit sorry for ourselves
We'll make this a Christmas to remember

Hidiho, we have just had an invite to go
And visit friends who live on the hill
Come and have Christmas with us
They said 'Eat, drink and be merry
 Indulge until you have had your fill.'

63   Chunky the Dinosaur

There once was a dinosaur called Chunky
Who was only a child aged four
He was so big that no one would play with him
Not even the children next door

He was as tall as a double Decker bus
His voice could be heard miles away
Mums feared that their children might get crushed
If they let them with Chunky play

He did feel very lonely
He admitted to himself that he was clumsy and large
He wanted to play with roller skates
But his feet were as large as a barge

Chunky's dad saw his son crying
When he came home from work one day
Dad worked very hard for his family
Despite the tax on his pay

'What's up son?' he asked
'I want some roller skates, Dad, but can't get any my size.'
Dad was very upset to see Chunky crying
And took a hanky and wiped his son's eyes

'Leave it to me, son, and I will see what I can do
But there must be a way.'
He didn't know what giant skates would cost
Though he was perfectly willing to pay

Dad spoke to his wife about their son Chunky
And wondered just what they could do
Then Dad had a bright idea and went and bought some hay carts
Not one but two

When Chunky saw them he went mad and said
'You have made me happy and glad.'
He tied them on to Chunky's feet
'Do they fit you son?' asked Dad

'Eh Dad, I think they're champion
No other kids have skates like mine."
So off he went down the hill faster than all the rest
And up a steep incline

'Dee Da Dee Da' the sound of a police car
Coming behind made him stop
'Young man you were going faster than we were,'
Said a blue-eyed, fair-haired cop

'I am sorry, sir,' said Chunky, trying not to laugh
'I got these skates for my birthday.'
'I don't care, rules are made to be obeyed
You can't speed on the Queen's highway.'

'Now over yonder is a disused motorway
Why don't you go and play on that?'
This made Chunky happy
He thanked them, and went off waving his hat

The miles of motorway on which to skate
Gave Chunky room to play
There's no report that he has been seen
So he may even be skating today

64 Rationing

Do you remember the old days
Of the ration books, and long queues?
If we had the same again today
My mother would turn to booze

Two rashers of bacon, a person, a week
Two ounces of lard, and butter
Two ounces of tea per person
You could hear the shoppers mutter

Clothes were rationed, so were sweets
But somehow we seemed to get by
We got used to rationing for everyday things
But to scrounge a little extra, we'd try

Word got around a boat had come in
The shops were selling fresh fruit
We'd race down town in the hundreds
Always taking the shortest route

If my old mum could see the stores today
Stacked out with every conceivable thing
Like Sainsbury, Asda and Tesco
She'd be first in the queue in the morning

65   The Antique Fair

Parked to capacity
Antiques abound
Shuffling seeking crowds
Bumping-apologising
Many to look
A few to buy

Pick it up
Put it down, walk on
Dealers snoozing
Chatting, reading
Ignoring punters
Complaining of
A lousy fair

Much to see
Particularly pretty
Pieces of porcelain
Paintings and paraphernalia
Bartering, dealing
Offers accepted
A satisfactory sale

Feet are aching
Tired of browsing
Thirsty, hungry
Feeling confused
Purchased nothing
Time to call it
A day

66   Shadows

Long and short
Dark and grey
Can hold secrets
We can't see
Fear of the unknown
Make us rest uneasy

In contrast, shade
Cool relaxing, discarded
Garments of the sun
Laid out
Like Raleigh's cloak
For our comfort

A noise in a shadow
Someone there?
Fear, sweat
Call again, no answer
Alone, no help
Flesh cold and clammy

Shadows lengthen
Moon is waning
Shadows blend with night
Tomorrow start again
Light and shadow
Hand in hand

67   The Family Tree

Have I told you that I'm on a diet and really trying hard to slim
It's not the first time, I admit to that
And I don't want to go down the gym

I haven't set a target and have tried not to boast to my friends
I have been at it now for near three weeks
And it is becoming a trend

I must admit I do feel better for it: the jowls round my chin have gone
I don't eat cakes and when I go out for a cup of tea
I forfeit the scone

I did have a shock today when I treated myself to some scales
Only to find that when I trod on them
The pointer went off the rails

To say I was shocked puts it mildly: I didn't know I was so large
It put me in mind of that comment once heard
That I was as big as a barge

It really is no laughing matter because I am type one diabetic as well
And even though I am careful
The injections have made my tummy swell

I eat sensibly and have only a small glass of wine with my dinner
I don't eat chips or fry-ups
So with that and exercise I should be slimmer

My granddad was a a big man, so was my dad and baby brother like me
I am beginning to have second thoughts
That I'm just a branch of the family tree

68   Moose International

Moose International used to be called
The Loyal Order of Moose
Named after that Canadian animal
Living wild and roaming loose

The reason why they chose the name
Was because it was big and brave
Secondly it was a family beast
It was a hero – it wasn't afraid

Comprised of ordinary men and women
Plus all of God's little children too
The Moose is there to look after them all
Without it, what would we all do?

The Mooseheart is the hub of it all
It's a large comfy house like a home
Where Moose from all over the world
Can feel at ease, to relax, and roam

They don't practise outdated rituals
No funny handshakes to grasp
Or passwords to try and remember
All of that is a thing of the past

Though the numbers are decreasing
And the majority left, getting old
Don't let it be said they are giving in
And that they are going to fold

They are here to look after the old
And to look after the children too
Many members are widowed
Of those there are quite a few

Yes they do need new members
There's nothing unusual in that
They raise vast amounts for charity
So throw some money into the hat

69   Alphabetically Speaking

Hello, how are you – Aye?
Fine, I live in Cardigan Bay
It's alright but lots of Clay
I come here every Day
Today though I am very Earlay
Here he comes, my friend Faye
Yes, that's right we are both Gay
It's nice to romp together in the Hay

Just seen the dentist, had an Inlay
That bird over there, isn't it a Jay?
I don't know, ask my friend Kay
How many eggs, Fay, does a jay Lay?
I don't know but they lay in May
That's not the answer is it? Nay
Ask Ray, the tall one he's OK
Come for a drink gang? I'll Pay

I will meet you all by the Quay
Fay says that your name is Ray
Oh Ray you're Scottish, you don't Say
Scotland's nice I like the Tay
I have to buy a new Underlay
My old one hurts my Vertebray
It's no trouble it's on my Way
Poor Fay she has to have an X-ray
Ask her if she's well, she says Yea
Come for a drink. Ray, what d'you Zay?

70   Dad Has Tiled the Bathroom

Father has just tiled the bathroom
You never seen such a mess
He's got filler all over his trousers
And some on mother's best dress

The tiles are stuck on with glue
Not the proper stuff from the store
He's used some stuff called Araldite
But that's not what it was intended for

The tiles look wonky and out of line
The gaps between them are massive
Why he chose purple I'll never know
He says it makes him feel passive

Peter my brother, says he won't bath again
Not that he needs an excuse not to
I wish Dad wouldn't bother with DIY
He's even tried tiling the loo

He's attempted to put sealant around the bath
It really is one hell of a sight
There's white sticky stuff on the purple tiles
And he's even got some on the light

71   Mother's Home Cooking

I love the cakes my mum used to make
Her apple pies with cloves in too
I don't know how she found the time to bake
And she made fantastic oxtail stew

I remember in the Second World War
When ingredients were in short supply
She used to make big cakes galore
Using burnt sugar, from the stove, as a dye

She would make one for my teacher
And an old lady who lived up the road
She always remembered the preacher
Her skill from the pulpit he crowed

I would come down from my bedroom
And on the kitchen table would find
A large fruitcake and some small ones
Some iced, and decorated, with rind

I remember, once I raced home from school
Hoping to find cakes in the tin
I was loading my pockets up like a pig
When my eldest sister walked in

I slammed the door with its glass pane
And taunted my sister outside
Annoyed, she banged hard on the glass
Yelling, she smashed it, I was surprised

A large gash in her arm was the result
She still carries the large scar today
I'm ashamed of myself for what I did
For her forgiveness I shall always pray

72 Nanny

What a wonderful feeling to be a nanny
Especially for the very first time
I was pleased when she was named Sophie
Wouldn't have minded if she were mine

No one was bothered what sex baby was
As long as both were healthy and fine
Her dad was as proud as a peacock
Though it wasn't a boy, he didn't mind

I remember the night the baby was born
Everyone's nerves were on end
I was awake at three in the morning
My services I was willing to lend

Sophie is now nearly seven years old
She has a sister who is her best mate
Both very pretty girls and full of life
The name of her sister is Kate

73   The Victorian Party

To dress up or not was the question?
It had to have a Victorian flavour
When I suggested I go as the Prince Consort
My wife said, 'Do me a favour.'

So she dressed me in an old blazer of mine
And selected a shirt that I hate
When she wanted to paint a moustache on my lip
I said, 'You know what you can do mate.'

We went to the party, most friends were there
The Mayor and his lady came too
Rita was dressed as Victoria
Les Fautley had just cleaned the flue

All the ladies looked adorable
They'd made every effort to please
The food they laid on was a credit to them
There was chicken, rolls, biscuits and cheese

A lantern slide just like the old days
A singer and piano too
We all enjoyed a wonderful night
I won a raffle prize too!

Well done to those who arranged the show
It was a credit to them, I'm sure
One appreciates the work that goes into it
We love it, can we have more?

74   Boys Will Always Be Boys

I feel I must relate for the record
Though much of it would be frowned on today
The things boys did years ago for kicks
But 'Boys will be boys,' they used to say

Bows and arrows, cut from trees in the woods
Trolleys from boxes, and wheels from a pram
Catapults, with leather from an old shoe
Hot loaves from the bakers, covered with jam

Climbing trees in the woods, doing no damage
Running errands for the old and infirm
Bird nesting was fun, from a nest we took one
Especially in holidays and at half term

No drugs, no graffiti, no raping old ladies
We got whacked by the teacher at school
Boy scouts carried knives on their belts in those days
We got whacked for breaking Mum's rules

75   Talking to Mum

Do you want a cup of tea, Mother?
Plus a nice fresh buttered bun
There's only two left in the packet
And I have already eaten one

Can I fluff up the cushion for you, Mother?
Just like I have done for years
Then brush and comb your grey locks
Though they're getting thin I fear

Shall I get your slippers for you, Mother?
And slip them on your feet
Don't get up, Mother, I'll answer the door
It could be Fred or Aunt Beat

Shall we go to the pictures tonight, Mother?
Instead of us watching the telly?
Or we could go to bingo, for a change
With Bert and Jean and Aunt Nelly

I really must stop talking like this
Though it has gone on for many years
It's just that I am missing you, Mother
And I can't hold back the tears

76   The Scout Family

I couldn't ignore the scouting movement
When I was a boy, even if I wanted to
They are so much a part of everyday life
Like milkmen and postmen
Young men who wanted to help
Who asked no reward but would like
A bob for a job
My father was a scout

Never in scandal unless inflicted on them
The pure Christian youth of today and tomorrow
Dressed in green jumpers
With badges sewn on and shorts with brown legs
Complete with bandana and woggle
Trustworthy enough to carry a sheathed knife
In their belt, never to be used flippantly or in anger
I was a scout

No better model citizen can be found
An example to the shooting, stabbing youth of today
They respect their parents, the old and infirm
They know and obey the countryside code
And are independent, reliable, fun loving
As they still are today
Round their campfires at night
They sing the songs of Baden-Powell's day
My son is a scout

77   The Ladies' Group

I must tell you about a ladies' group
Who meet once every two weeks
I'll change the names of those concerned
So they can't blame me for my cheek

Well, first there's old Mrs Wotsit
She gave us a biscuit with tea
You might say that's very kind of her
But she charged us ninety-nine pee

Then there is a big woman
I nicknamed her Posh Spice
Poor dear says she never feels well
But her figure is very nice

Next there is a stout woman
Who is an authority on poetry
She is talented, and she knows it
Though she suffers from bardolotry

That Mrs Whosit, she seldom comes
She just loves to hear her own voice
She has a habit of upsetting the group
I would ban her if I had the choice

I used to be the club secretary
But they talked about me all the time
So I left and took up knitting instead
For their companionship I don't pine

78   The Evacuee

I was a little boy of ten years old
When Hitler sent to me
A ten ton bomb as a present
It flattened my house and a tree
I wasn't the only child you see
To have a gift from him
The family next door are no more
The outlook appeared very grim

So I had to leave London town
An adventure was about to begin
I had to travel by train to Devon
Where war had still never been
The bus turned up right on time
Tearfully we said our goodbye
My brother and sister were with me
We had sandwiches and a meat pie

I had never seen a train before
It hissed and gave off steam
It looked like a big steel monster
To drive one must be a dream
Eight of us kids to a carriage
There wasn't much room to sit
I grabbed a seat by the window
A bit squashed, but I managed to fit

It was a very long journey
We were tired and wanted a meal
Nothing to do but sit and talk
Homesickness, I began to feel
We stopped at a station in Devon
Whose name I now forget
Loads of people there to greet us
We chose Uncle Fred and Margaret

They treated us just like their own
We went to church on Sunday
Played football at school in the week
In summer romped in the hay
We were happy where we were living
The people there were very kind
But I can't wait until the war's over
And can leave lovely Devon behind

79   Grandpa's Shed

There is a place grandpa loves
Second only to his bed
A hut at the bottom of the garden
We call grandpa's shed
I don't know what is in it
I have never been allowed to see
Grandma says, that what goes on
Is one big mystery

The window is so dirty
You cannot see inside
The door it is supported
By a plank that's two foot wide
I've tried spying through the keyhole
But that's all bunged up too
I'e tried prodding with a skewer
To improve the view

I think he's up to no good
Why be secretive like that
When questioned he replies
'No questions and you will hear no lies'
There is whirring and banging
The radio blares Channel Two
I'd love to know what he's doing
I bet that you would too

80   Nearly in Heaven

Various shades of blue flash before my eyes, moving laterally at various speeds. Intermixed with these are greens, whites and black. I saw them, even though I'm colour blind.

These colours were those of the different uniforms worn by the many trades and professions that go to make up the nursing team on a hospital ward; each person is a trained asset to the job of getting people better.

They, together with the immaculately clean ward I was bedded in, gave me a great assurance that they were all only interested in me and my welfare, and that their priority was to get me better as quickly and efficiently as possible.

The comfort and near luxury of my surroundings made me realise how lucky I was to get the finest treatment 24/7.

Nothing was too much trouble. My every need was either already clocked into a tight set schedule; or was granted on the mere press of a bedside bell and it wasn't costing me a penny.

Meanwhile the doctors, many of whom were younger than my grandchildren, orchestrated the running of the entire operation. They had their fingers literally on the pulse of every patient in their care. Although few in number, these young doctors were skilled at getting people better.

Index

About the author

Bill Jackman has been in the antique trade, buying, selling and collecting for 45 years. He has written numerous articles for the press and antique magazines, and has lectured on Georgian glass to dozens of Probus clubs, U3As, and other associations in the southwest of England. He is a member of the Glass Society, Silver Society and the Society of Authors.

His two books on antiques are *Masonic Memorabilia for Collectors* (Gemini Publications Ltd, 2002), an illustrated price guide which has sold well all over the world and *Investing Investing in Antique Silver Toys and Miniatures* (AESOP Publications, 2011).

He has written and published five poetry books (all proceeds donated to charity) and has written plays and a six-part situation comedy based on caravanning. He has published one novel, *The Freemasons Daughter* (Authorhouse, 2009), and two further novels are in preparation.

Bill's military career

Bill was only eleven when he started his army career. He went away in 1947 to the Duke of York's Royal Military School in Dover Kent. He stayed there for three years because he was keen to become a naval artificer, but failed because he was colour blind. He next went to the Army Apprentice College, Arborfield, Berks in 1951. He served a three-year apprenticeship and passed out of the college and joined the REME where he served for 22 years, filling every rank from Craftsman to Artificer Sergeant Major. He gained medals in Malaya and Aden and served also in Korea, Japan, Hong Kong, Cyprus, Singapore and Europe. He retired in 1976 and went into selling catering equipment to hotels, pubs and restaurants.

Bill lives with his wife Jinty in Weston-super-Mare.

Lightning Source UK Ltd.
Milton Keynes UK
UKOW041044220312

189403UK00001B/19/P